A REUNION
OF STRANGERS

Words of Wisdom from the
FAMILIES IN GLOBAL TRANSITION
Conference Community

Celebrating 20 years
of diverse mobile lives

First published in 2018 by Summertime Publishing

Copyright Summertime Publishing 2018

ISBN: 978-1-9998808-0-4

Compiled by Marijne Nieuwerf

Edited by Ginny Philps

Designed by Creationbooth.com

Acknowledgements

Many thanks to Marijne Nieuwerf, who conducted the research necessary to compile these quotes. Marijne's work took her right back to the earliest days of Families in Global Transition (FIGT) in 1998 in Indianapolis.

Ongoing thanks are due to the FIGT community as a whole. Spanning the globe, and diverse in age, background and motivation, it is the members themselves who give the transient life an identity and value of its own.

To those present at the FIGT conferences, who actively capture the sessions and share via social media for those unable to attend.

Many thanks to Jo Parfitt, who established the Parfitt-Pascoe Writing Residency (PPWR) initiative in 2014 to facilitate the documentation of all future FIGT conferences and the training of budding writers to this end. It is through Jo's insistence on quality and honesty that the wealth of information created through these meetings is available for wider dissemination, ongoing reference, and lasting archives. This book of quotes represents a celebration of the 20th anniversary of Families in Global Transition.

Enduring thanks are due also to Robin Pascoe, for being there from the very early days of FIGT and, since 2017, for being fully engaged with supporting and funding the PPWR.

Preface

Apart from Ruth Van Reken, there can't be many people who have attended almost all the FIGT conferences. We have been there from close to the beginning, but sadly we missed the first two – including that first fledgling conference back in 1998, when the conference barely had a name, just a couple of keynotes and a choice of three concurrent sessions. Eighty-five people attended that first conference, almost half of them from in-state. Robin's first FIGT was 2000 and Jo's 2001. In March 2018 we celebrate 20 years since that first event, funded and hosted by Eli Lilly in Indianapolis. How things change. In 2017 a record 200 people attended a conference in The Hague, Netherlands and came from all over the world.

Robin and I are journalists and authors of several books on expatriate issues. Over the years we have led concurrent sessions, keynoted and enjoyed belonging to this unique reunion of strangers. We have met best friends we never knew before and have learned so much from the wisdom that has been shared, always willingly, always without an ulterior motive, not only by the speakers but also by the attendees. We rubbed shoulders with the greats of the expatriate world, the game-changers and those who invented the vocabulary we all use so easily today – Adult Third Culture Kid (ATCK), unresolved grief, global nomads, Spouses Travelling and Relocating Successfully (STARS), even Third Culture Adult (TCA) and Cross-Cultural Kid (CCK). As writers, we considered it our role to document what we learned at FIGT and to disseminate it as best we could, through our websites (Robin wrote prolifically at www.expatexpert.com, Jo at www.expatrollercoaster.com), for papers such as *The Wall Street Journal, The Independent on Sunday, The Weekly Telegraph, Mobility* and many more. Passionate about the generosity and wisdom that is to be found at these conferences we wrote as much as we could. Yet, it was never enough. Never enough to spread the word wide enough; as widely as it deserved.

This is why, in 2014, The Parfitt-Pascoe Writing Residency was formed. Now the words uttered at this 'reunion of strangers' can be documented and disseminated effectively through the *Insights and Interviews* series of books, their blogs and guestposts, while giving new writers the leg-up in their career that we received ourselves 30, 40 years ago and for which we are always grateful.

The words you will enjoy here, along with those who first said them within the privileged walls of the FIGT conference, will, we hope, give you a taste of what this great conference is all about. May this book inspire us to continue to share and write the words that will ensure FIGT continues to grow and be such a source of support and inspiration and, let's face it, friends, for all those who attend.

Jo Parfitt and Robin Pascoe
January 2018

Contents

"A reunion of strangers,"

Dr Norma McCaig, founder of Global Nomads, is cited as having first described FIGT by this term

A REUNION OF STRANGERS

– 1 –

Moving with Children, Third Culture Kids

"[Internationally mobile individuals require] a flow of care... preparation for transition to overseas assignments, support while living and working cross-culturally, and preparation for re-entering one's home culture."

– *Dave Pollock, FIGT 1998, Indianapolis*

"The international school experience was incredibly rich for all our kids."

– *Peggy Love, FIGT 2012, Washington*

"I realised I had experienced more by the ninth grade than many people do in a lifetime, and I was still standing, which meant I was strong."

– *Elizabeth Liang, FIGT 2014, Washington*

"Third Culture Kids (TCKs) can be the next problem solvers with the right tools and support."

— Ellen Mahoney, FIGT 2014, Washington

"To most expats, the only permanent thing is change."

— Kristine Racina, FIGT 2014, Washington

"One of the most effective ways to [create an enhanced sense of security] is by giving TCKs a platform or voice to share their experiences and express any frustrations."

— Kate Berger, FIGT 2014, Washington

"I know what it is like to transition between countries, go to boarding school for the majority of my education, attempt to adjust back to my home country as a teenager and not feel at home anywhere."

— Lois Bushong, FIGT 2014, Washington

"We need to broaden our research. With increasing mobility in the world, the study of globally mobile people must also grow. It is important not only for TCKs, Cross-Cultural Kids (CCKs), and other expats to know themselves, but the static communities they participate in can also benefit from having a better understanding of them."

— Ann Baker Cottrell, FIGT 2015, Washington

"Much is given to those lucky enough to experience a life moving across cultures, particularly during their developmental years. But these individuals must be able to *cope* with all they have been given for it to be good for them."

– *Doug Ota, FIGT 2015, Washington*

"The global journey is experiencing life on the outside."

– *Trisha Carter, FIGT 2016, Amsterdam*

"Transition is about leaving a *place* and settling into a *space*, which one must then sculpt in to a new place."

– *Kathleen Swords, FIGT 2016, Amsterdam*

"All members of the family will have different perspectives. The goal is to respect that, and try to understand."

– Ruth Van Reken, FIGT 2016, Amsterdam

"Look at what is already working and build on it, even if it is just a tiny piece. Connect your child to the one thing that is okay among all the change."

– Kristin Duncombe, FIGT 2017, The Hague

"Recognising that your child's identity may be different from your own is one of the most important things that parents of global and mobile kids need to get their heads around. When you raise your kids in a way that is different from the way you have been raised, in a country that is different from the country in which you have been raised, they don't turn out to be just little photocopies of yourself. They turn out to be people with different identities."

— *Kristin Duncombe, FIGT 2017, The Hague*

"Every place that you live adds quality to your life."

— *Sebastien Bellin, FIGT 2017, The Hague*

"Early Muslims used camels, but we use aeroplanes."

– Maryam Afnan Ahmad, FIGT 2017, The Hague

"You do not have to move abroad to experience culture shock."

– Olga Mecking, FIGT 2017, The Hague

"I recommend that TCKs take a gap year."

– Cliff Gardner, FIGT 2017, The Hague

– 2 –

Adult Third Culture Kids

"I certainly believe that being an expat can make a person more aware of one's blessings."

– Pico Iyer, FIGT 2004, Dallas

"We are TCAs (Third Culture Adults)."

– Paulette Bethel, FIGT 2009, Houston

"The places in which I have lived have left indelible marks on me. In some ways I feel like I carry parts of each place inside myself, whether I am living in Kenya, Senegal or DC."

– Dr. Fanta Aw, FIGT 2014, Washington

"Being raised as a TCK makes you feel that everything is temporary – you know your place in the world is not going to last, so you don't commit to it."

– Nina Sichel, FIGT 2015, Washington

"TCKs are in a unique position to teach empathy; stereotypes are a lazy way to see others."

– Tayo Rockson, FIGT 2015, Washington

"TCKs are good at adaptability, seeing multiple perspectives and there are no whole truths. They have mixed loyalty if forced to choose a side."

– Antje Rauwerda, FIGT 2015, Washington

"'I chose to celebrate my differences,'" he said. " 'I learned there was beauty in the diverse world we live in.'" Why not use your difference to *make* a difference?"

– Tayo Rockson, FIGT 2015, Washington

"Honour your voice. Honour your family. Honour what you do."

– Trisha Carter and Rachel Yates, FIGT 2015, Washington

"The concept of *story* is really critical for our TCKs."

– Susan Murray, FIGT 2016, Amsterdam

"Stories are powerful; they should not be in the margins. There needs to be an amplification of the marginal voices."

– Mary Bassey, FIGT 2016, Amsterdam

"Stories shape us. We are not here randomly."

– Ruth Van Reken, FIGT 2016, Amsterdam

"We have a world of people who don't know who they are."

– Ruth Van Reken, FIGT 2016, Amsterdam

"We are increasingly international, but we all live local lives."

– Dr. Rachel Cason, FIGT 2016, Amsterdam

"TCKs develop a relationship to *place* that is embedded but transitory."

– Dr. Rachel Cason, FIGT 2016, Amsterdam

"*Place* represents resource as well as challenge."

– Dr. Rachel Cason, FIGT 2016, Amsterdam

"Identity props such as language, food and local relationships may be employed to increase connectedness between the fragmented elements of a TCK's history."

– Dr. Rachel Cason, FIGT 2016, Amsterdam

"Place has the potential to ground our histories and offer coherence to the present, thus facilitating greater Settledness of Self."

– Dr. Rachel Cason, FIGT 2016, Amsterdam

"The more intimate the story, the more universal."

– Melissa Dalton-Bradford, FIGT 2016, Amsterdam

"Tell your stories! Because that's the thing about being a TCK — we hide who we are in order to adapt. Stories are far better and are more resilient."

– Janneke Muyselaar-Jellema, FIGT 2017, The Hague

"I never felt so foreign as when I was surrounded by people who thought I was one of them."

– Maria Lombart, FIGT 2017, The Hague

"As TCKs grow up, we learn quickly that to say goodbye is an expected part of life. We leave without a tear because we know there will be many more goodbyes ahead."

– Maria Lombart, FIGT 2017, The Hague

– 3 –

The Concept of *Home*

"It's that constant feeling of 'I don't need a geographical place, but I do need a people place... a space, not geographically, not in time, but a space in which I can find myself.'"

– Kira Miller Fabregat, FIGT 2000, Indianapolis

"I wish that other adults without global experience would understand that the US is not home."

– Unknown in teen panel, FIGT 2007, Houston

"Home is a concept not a place."

– Unknown in teen panel, FIGT 2007, Houston

"My home is a plane that drops me into new places."

– Julia Simens, FIGT 2014, Washington

"I have learned that 'where is home?' and 'where are you from?' are two very different questions, but they both are part of what one defines as home."

– Valérie Besanceney, FIGT 2015, Washington

"I feel rooted among the people I love, regardless of where we happen to be. I am probably more rooted in relationships than I am in particular places."

– Nina Sichel, FIGT 2015, Washington

"Home to me is more of an emotional connection than one singular place."

– Tashi Nibber, FIGT 2015, Washington

"No matter where I was, as long as I was with people, it was a family."

– Lydia Foxall, FIGT 2016, Amsterdam

– 4 –

Belonging

"We are a universe of strangers. You can feel closer to people here than you do your own relatives."

– Matt Neigh, FIGT 2007, Houston

"I'm not from a place, I'm from people."

– Elizabeth Liang, FIGT 2014, Washington

"Expats arrive at their new destination culturally naked."

– Chris O'Shaughnessy, FIGT 2016, Amsterdam

"The feeling of not belonging goes hand in hand with all the amazing things that we have because we are on this global journey."

— *Trisha Carter, FIGT 2016, Amsterdam*

"We welcome you a stranger, send you back home a friend."

— *Wilhelm Post, FIGT 2017, The Hague*

"Languages don't divide, they bring families together."

— *Rita Rosenback, FIGT 2017, The Hague*

– 5 –

Identity

"When a spouse marries into the military, she has little choice, but needs to be educated to understand what her choice means *before* she gets married."

– *Scott Keehn, FIGT 2002, Indianapolis*

"See your assignment as a living laboratory for growth and transformation."

– *Barbara Schaetti, FIGT 2004, Dallas*

"My professional identity is very important to me. I have always refused to be 'just a' anything."

– *Jo Parfitt, FIGT 2007, Houston*

"Cultural marginality is a cultural lifestyle at the edges where two or more cultures meet [...] by maintaining control of choice and the construction of boundaries, a person may become a *constructive* marginal [...] able to construct context intentionally and consciously for the purpose of creating his or her own identity."

– Dr Janet Bennet, FIGT 2007, Houston

"Defining our identity based on our personal language does away with having to define ourselves with black and white concepts. Such concepts can cause confusion or upheaval every time we grow or become more aware of various aspects of ourselves in the past."

– Myra Dumapias, FIGT 2014, Washington

"I believe that there are multiple selves that we occupy from place to place."

– Brittani Sonnenberg, FIGT 2015, Washington

"Languages unite. They do not divide.
They bring families together."

– Rita Rosenback, FIGT 2017, The Hague

– 6 –

Career and Business

"The wife makes the choice when she marries a diplomat in the first place."

– Robin Pascoe, FIGT 2002, Indianapolis

"We have up until last week been known as 'trailing spouses', to my mind a rather derogatory tag, though slightly better than EFMs (eligible family member) which was coined by the US State Department. Now we, men and women, are to be known as *STARS – Spouses Travelling and Relocating Successfully*. This was decreed by attendees of the conference from across all sectors, military, diplomatic, academic, NGO and corporate, as well as the service providers and those of us who follow."

– Apple Gidley, FIGT 2011, Washington

"If you don't know how to do everything, do the one thing that you can do."

– *Ruth Van Reken, FIGT 2016, Amsterdam*

"Try the thing that carries the greatest risk, because it also has the most potential."

– *Kilian Kröll, FIGT 2017, The Hague*

"Go out into the world and do something."

– *Cristina Baldan and Claudia Baldini, FIGT 2017, The Hague*

– 7 –

Grief and Loss

"Grief is a messy, backward and forward process."

– Doug Ota, FIGT 2009, Houston

"Grieving is the painful gift that allows us to turn walls into ladders, such that something that once split us in half becomes a ladder by which we climb to a higher order of coherence, and our world becomes bigger. Like the way a bone heals stronger where it has been broken, these breaks in our story, as painful as they can be, pave the way to a hardier wholeness."

– Doug Ota, FIGT 2009, Houston

"The joy doesn't negate the pain of the loss, and the pain of chronic cycles of separation and loss don't negate the joy. Never ever forget you only grieve for losing something you loved."

– Ruth Van Reken, FIGT 2014, Washington

"Grief is the work that it takes to glue back together the pieces of our story so that they make some semblance of sense."

– Doug Ota, FIGT 2009, Houston

"Accept the challenges and grief that come with this lifestyle, because once you do, the advantages will become all the more clearer."

– Valérie Besanceney, FIGT 2015, Washington

"We get home by being able to say goodbye."

– Doug Ota, FIGT 2015, Washington

"The purpose of rituals is to separate one phase of life from the next. Besides a funeral, what are the rituals for goodbye?"

– Doug Ota, FIGT 2015, Washington

"The experience of being understood is the best healing."

– Doug Ota, FIGT 2015, Washington

"The hero has to say goodbye in order to eventually come home."

– Doug Ota, FIGT 2015, Washington

"Where we are broken is where we bond."

– *Melissa Dalton-Bradford, FIGT 2016, Amsterdam*

"[Some] experiences are so beautiful because we know the loss that went into [them]."

– *Melissa Dalton-Bradford, FIGT 2016, Amsterdam*

– 8 –

Tribes, Networking and Community

"No matter how sophisticated a traveller may be, everyone needs a helping hand when settling into a new community."

– Pam Perraud, FIGT 2002, Indianapolis

"You have to go with the flow. You have to be positive about it."

– Jane Smith, FIGT 2007, Houston

"Make new friends, but keep the old. One is silver, the other gold."

– Sandy Thomas, FIGT 2009, Houston

"We live in a web of interconnected relationships. *Family* is people who we claim and who claim us. The people who show up."

– Dr. Fanta Aw, FIGT 2014, Washington

"One adult outside your parents who believes in you can make such a difference."

– Ellen Mahoney, FIGT 2014, Washington

"Not only did everyone understand what living a mobile life was about, but everyone was passionate about helping others who are struggling because of it."

– Danau Tanu, FIGT 2014, Washington

"Our responsibility to empower the global family goes beyond getting them through their next overseas assignment. It now stretches to bringing better chances of success long term, as well as a sense of meaning to global life."

— Ray S. Leki, FIGT 2014, Washington

"Be determined to do the next right thing. We can't handle all of it, all of the time. But we can focus on doing the next right thing."

— Becky Grappo, FIGT 2014, Washington

"When people come to you for help and advice, share with them. Put your good stuff out in to the universe."

— Patricia Linderman, FIGT 2015, Washington

"Don't just look for community –
create it!"

– Chris O'Shaughnessy, FIGT 2015, Washington

"Every interaction gives or
takes life. There are no neutral
interactions."

– Chris O'Shaughnessy, FIGT 2016, Amsterdam

"Everyone has a place at the table –
we just need to pull out the chairs."

– Mary Bassey, FIGT 2016, Amsterdam

"The people give us what we become."

– Marielle de Spa, FIGT 2017, The Hague

"We have a responsibility not to focus so much on *our* programme but to actually look at our community – the transition in and the transition out. To [consider] our duty in working with other communities to ensure our Tribe are looked after when they leave our community."

– Claudine Hakim, FIGT 2017, The Hague

"We need three things to build a Tribe: a smile, an open mind and patience."

– Naomi Hattaway, FIGT 2017, The Hague

"I have experiences and wisdom to share with my community. I am what I am because of who *we* are together."

— *Naomi Hattaway, FIGT 2017, The Hague*

"Every single Tribe has its own mindset because of the circumstances and the journey they have lived."

— *Marielle de Spa, FIGT 2017, The Hague*

"Not experiencing community is not an option."

— *Naomi Hattaway, FIGT 2017, The Hague*

"I am filled with encouragement and hope at the thought of a community of people who will be at the forefront, leading the world into the increasingly global future."

– Hannele Secchia, FIGT 2017, The Hague

"I now know more than ever that I am not alone on this journey."

– Hannele Secchia, FIGT 2017, The Hague

– 9 –

Elder Care

"Just because you aren't there,
doesn't mean you don't care."

*– Dr. Jill Kristal and Elizabeth Vennekens-Kelly, FIGT
2014, Washington*

"If you have left so many times, you
learn not to attach yourself too
much."

*– College-age TCKs from 1994, 2001 and 2014, FIGT
2015, Washington*

"It's the emotional distance that
counts, not the physical distance."

– Kathleen Swords, FIGT 2016, Amsterdam

– 10 –

Technology

"I am very grateful for the invention of email to be able to stay in regular contact with friends."

– College-age TCKs from 1994, 2001 and 2014, FIGT 2015, Washington

"With Skype it's so easy to stay in touch; it's almost like we're still together."

– College-age TCKs from 1994, 2001 and 2014, FIGT 2015, Washington

"It makes sense that empathy is decreasing as technology increases, but technology facilitates travel which [in itself] can increase empathy."

– Grant Simens, FIGT 2015, Washington

"With things like iMessage and Snapchat you can pick up where you left off when you see friends again."

– College-age TCKs from 1994, 2001 and 2014, FIGT 2015, Washington

"The reason I blog today is that it helps me connect with all of you. It is the best thing I could have done, and I don't know what took me so long."

– Mariam Ottimofiore, FIGT 2017, The Hague

– 11 –

Creativity

"Problems are just opportunities in disguise."

– Jo Parfitt, FIGT 2001, Indianapolis

"Interestingly, it is when in prison or other enforced solitary confinement (and when new in town loneliness can be acute), that this lack of communication and connection with others can lead us to create our own ways of expression. For me, this has been with words. Many prisoners are inspired to write for the first time during their time 'inside'."

– Jo Parfitt, FIGT 2007, Houston

"Words are really powerful. All words, in a way, are metaphors for trying to understand our own experiences."

– Josh Sandoz, FIGT 2010, Houston

"Creativity isn't based on what you're born with. It's what's left over after being killed off by parents and teachers."

– *Dr. Kyung Hee Kim, FIGT 2014, Washington*

"What's your dream or passion? Find others of like-mindedness, then create and enlarge your network."

– *Ruth Van Reken, FIGT 2016, Amsterdam*

"It's not a matter of ambition or being greedy. It's a matter of saying: 'I have talent and I want to contribute.'"

– *Alix Carnot, FIGT 2017, The Hague*

– 12 –

Personal Development, Resilience and Curiosity

"No matter where you go in life, always unpack your bags and plant your trees... maybe you won't be there to eat the fruit from those trees, but someone else will."

– Ruth Van Reken, speaking her father, Charles Frame's, words, FIGT 2014, Washington

"Emotional resilience is essential for everyone, but especially so for those living a mobile, cross-cultural, global life."

– Linda A. Janssen, FIGT 2014, Washington

"Remarriage across cultures requires extra determination. It's about relationships – maintaining the existing ones and building new ones."

– Dr. Jill Kristal and Elizabeth Vennekens-Kelly, FIGT 2014, Washington

"The biggest obstacle to reaching your dream is you."

– Ellen Mahoney, FIGT 2014, Washington

"We should all be honest and open about the risks of depression after relocation, and we all need to take extra steps to keep ourselves emotionally healthy – exercising, seeking out positive social interactions, getting enough sleep, and finding fun, interesting new things to do."

– Patricia Linderman, FIGT 2015, Washington

"It's good to adjust. It's good to integrate. But it's important not to forget who you are."

– Geremie Sawadogo, FIGT 2015, Washington

"Use your smile to change the world, but don't let the world change your smile."

– Birgit Kuschel, FIGT 2015, Washington

"The most important thing to take with you [overseas] is yourself."

– Anonymous, FIGT 2015, Washington

"When I stop fighting with my expat life and start dancing instead, that's when it works."

– Cristina Bertarelli, FIGT 2015, Washington

"A person who is ready to explore his feelings is ready to explore his life."

– Doug Ota, FIGT 2015, Washington

"You're a blank sheet and you're filling that in."

– Niels Ota, FIGT 2015, Washington

"One of the keys to resilience is belonging to a bigger family story."

– Marilyn Gardner, FIGT 2016, Amsterdam

"Bring what you have. Every individual sitting in this room has a strength that can help someone in crisis."

— Melissa Dalton-Bradford, FIGT 2016, Amsterdam

"Celebrate when others build on your dream and do a better job than you did or can. Don't be jealous. You have a part. We all have parts."

— Ruth Van Reken, FIGT 2016, Amsterdam

"We know that being empathic and encouraging is a big motivator for those who are not as experienced as we are."

— Claudia Landini, FIGT 2016, Amsterdam

"You are all builders and architects."

– Emmy McCarthy, FIGT 2016, Amsterdam

"Try the thing that has the greatest risk because it also has the most potential."

– Kilian Kröll, FIGT 2017, The Hague

"The major life skill is to take the perspective of others."

– Dr. Anne Copeland, FIGT 2017, The Hague

"Fear is an illusion – it doesn't exist. Our minds make it a reality. Why allow fear to be part of your mindset?"

– Sebastien Bellin, FIGT 2017, The Hague

"Do you rebuild yourself on negativity or positivity?"

– Sebastien Bellin, FIGT 2017, The Hague

"Once you lay out your needs, you can find options."

– Dana Bachar Grossman, FIGT 2017, The Hague

"Curiosity was my tool, but knowledge was my goal."

– Basma al Rawi, FIGT 2017, The Hague

– 13 –

Other Tough Stuff

"Don't say goodbye to the people that matter. It's important to make an effort to stay in contact with and see friends."

– Grant Simens, FIGT 2015, Washington

"If we are too scared of invading someone's privacy and connecting, there are no conduits for hope to flow."

– Chris O'Shaugnessy, FIGT 2015, Washington

"The more quality you have in your life, the more you have to draw from in challenging times."

– Sebastien Bellin, FIGT 2017, The Hague

"My hope is that, by having the courage to speak frankly and honestly about my own struggles in the transitions in my life, I can free my reader, and the audiences I speak to, to do the same."

– Doug Ota, FIGT 2015, Washington

"Life overseas is not always a warm hug and a kiss on both cheeks."

– Naomi Hattaway, FIGT 2017, The Hague

– 14 –

Global Citizens

"We just have to think about global living in a more soulful way, which means having a global conscience and sense of responsibility."

– Pico Iyer, FIGT 2004, Dallas

"The whole world is singing Lady GaGa... with different accents."

– Pico Iyer, FIGT 2013, Maryland

"The reality, in a global lifestyle, is that some things are unknowable... some aspects of on-the-ground reality that you cannot control eight months ahead of time from 6000 miles away."

– Ray S. Leki, FIGT 2014, Washington

"As we enter cultures, we are not just learning how to adapt to a culture. We are learning to adapt to that culture's people, too."

– *Geremie Sawadogo, FIGT 2015, Washington*

"Every time you move, your story is truncated. By sharing our stories, we can create greater coherence."

– *Michael Pollock, FIGT 2016, Amsterdam*

"A global village in which they feel safe to embrace both the excitement of exploring and adapting to a new culture."

– *Emmy McCarthy, FIGT 2016, Amsterdam*

"Speaking and reading in one's own language makes people feel at home."

– Claudia Landini, FIGT 2016, Amsterdam

"Choose a place where enough people are also different, who know what it is to be different."

– Cliff Gardner, FIGT 2017, The Hague

"It's not the destination but the joy of the journey."

– Terry Anne Wilson, FIGT 2017, The Hague

– 15 –

Diversity, Being Different

"If I have one goal in life, it is that I want to see a spouse invited not just to the first meeting but to all the subsequent ones when a new posting is under discussion."

– Robin Pascoe, FIGT 2002, Indianapolis

"If a female minority is on expat assignment, she has already been through the hoops. She has proved herself in many ways."

– Kendra Mirasol and Charisse Kosova, FIGT 2010, Houston

"The only thing that defines you is who you think you are."

– Eva László-Herbert, FIGT 2013, Maryland

"Diversity is the nature of the universe."

– Teja Arboleda, FIGT 2015, Washington

"The colour of your skin has no bearing on your culture... there can be no multicultural crayon."

– Teja Arboleda, FIGT 2015, Washington

"Focusing too much on *otherness* decreases empathy."

– Chris O'Shaughnessy, FIGT 2016, Amsterdam

"There are a lot of ways you can be different underneath."

– Ruth Van Reken, FIGT 2016, Amsterdam

"Inclusion is important no matter where you are."

– Ruth Van Reken, FIGT 2016, Amsterdam

"What you see may be different from what other people see."

– Dr. Anne Copeland, FIGT 2017, The Hague

"Deal with diversity to find workable solutions."

– Cristina Baldan and Claudia Baldini, FIGT 2017, The Hague

– 16 –

Charity, Volunteering and Giving Back

"We must find ways to apply and leverage our global nomad experience to benefit not only ourselves, but also our global community that gave us so much."

– Patricia Stokke, FIGT 2014, Washington

"Volunteering gives people a chance to create community. Volunteering is not just about giving; it is also about receiving."

– Deborah Valentine, FIGT 2017, The Hague

– 17 –

The FIGT Conference Itself

"A reunion of people you've never met."

— Anonymous, FIGT 2004, Dallas

"The best thing about FIGT is the openness to interact and learn that everyone brings. Secondly, it is always cathartic to meet people who are immediately able to understand our shared struggle to create life when it is so transitory. Thirdly, I am just blown away by the fabulous research, tools and services people are creating."

— Maryam Afnan Ahmad, FIGT 2014, Washington

"People are inspired and comforted by other people's stories. When we remind each other that we are all human, it reminds us that we are capable of anything."

— Ellen Mahoney, FIGT 2014, Washington

"This small, intimate gathering of about 150 people, inspired by Ruth Van Reken around her own kitchen table 18 years ago, is a homecoming. It's a place where you don't have to explain yourself, your background, or your differences – unless you want to. And since everyone in the room has a unique story to share, it's also the one place where everyone wants to hear it."

– Becky Grappo, FIGT 2015, Washington

"My hope for everyone at this conference is that they [...] cultivate opportunities in their lives to experience integration and purpose every day. We are in the position to have an enormous impact on the planet."

– Kilian Kröll, FIGT 2015, Washington

"One thing I know for sure about FIGT is that my personal highlights have always been unplanned and unexpected."

– Kilian Kröll, FIGT 2015, Washington

"The dictionary definition of a 'commencement' is literally 'the beginning of something'. I get goose bumps when I think about what it took for everyone in this room to get to this final moment of the conference – and all the doors that are just about to open."

– Kilian Kröll, FIGT 2016, Amsterdam

"We bring our best professional work to the table, in addition to an open heart, a calm ear and the willingness to let ourselves be changed by this three-day experience."

– Kilian Kröll, FIGT 2016, Amsterdam

"The real purpose of the conference – that of connecting; not only connecting with others, but with our inner selves."

– Hannele Secchia, FIGT 2017, The Hague

REFERENCES

Moving with Children; Third Culture Kids

Maryam Afnan Ahmad
The Muslim Expatriate Experience. Retrieved from Mariam Ottimofiore's blog <u>www.andthenwemovedto.com</u>, March 27, 2017.

Sebastien Bellin
Plenary Speech: *I Should Fear, But I Don't, So Why Do You?* FIGT Conference 2017. Retrieved from Mariam Ottimofiore's blog <u>www.andthenwemovedto.com</u>, March 27, 2017.

Ann Baker Cotterell
Concurrent Session: *Research Panel*, FIGT Conference 2015. Retrieved from *Insights and Interviews from the 2015 Families in Global Transition (FIGT) Conference* (p. 119), Summertime Publishing, 2016.

Kate Berger
Kitchen Table Conversation: *Identity in Context: A Psychological Perspective on Why Third Culture Kids Struggle to Answer 'Who Am I?'* FIGT Conference 2014. Retrieved from *Insights and Interviews from the 2014 Families in Global Transition (FIGT) Conference* (p. 161), Summertime Publishing, 2015.

Lois Bushong
Interviewed at FIGT Conference 2014. Retrieved from *Insights and Interviews from the 2014 Families in Global Transition (FIGT) Conference* (p.10),
Summertime Publishing, 2015.

Trisha Carter
Panel Discussion: *Is Belonging Overrated*? FIGT
Conference 2016. Retrieved from Olga Mecking's
blog www.europeanmama.com, March 15, 2016.

Kristin Duncombe
Retrieved from Jane Barron's blog:
www.globallygrounded.com, May 30, 2017.

Cliff Gardner
Panel Discussion: *Finding Your Niche: Connecting
a Multicultural Past to a Meaningful Present,*
FIGT Conference 2017. Retrieved from Mariam
Ottimofiore's blog www.andthenwemovedto.com,
March 27, 2017.

Elizabeth Liang
Interviewed at FIGT Conference 2014. Retrieved
from *Insights and Interviews from the 2014
Families in Global Transition (FIGT) Conference*
(p.31), Summertime Publishing, 2015.

Peggy Love
Interviewed by ACS International Schools at
FIGT Conference 2012. Retrieved from www.
youtube.com/watch?v=mJj7TMIzZSM

Ellen Mahoney
Ignite Session: *How mentoring helps Third
Culture Kids Transition into Adulthood,* FIGT
Conference 2014. Retrieved from *Insights and
Interviews from the 2014 Families in Global
Transition (FIGT) Conference* (p. 145),
Summertime Publishing, 2015.

Olga Mecking
Kitchen Table Conversation: *Tribes: How and Where To Find Them?* FIGT Conference 2017.

Doug Ota
Interviewed at FIGT Conference 2015. Retrieved from www.uydmedia.com, July 5, 2015.

Dave Pollock
Speaker at FIGT Conference 1998. Retrieved from www.interactionintl.org/whoisdavepollock.asp

Kristine Racina
Ignite Session: *The Only Permanent Thing is Change but do we Document it Appropriately?* FIGT Conference 2014. Retrieved from *Insights and Interviews from the 2014 Families in Global Transition (FIGT) Conference* (p. 148), Summertime Publishing, 2015.

Ruth Van Reken
Retrieved from Marilyn Gardner's blog www.communicatingacrossboundariesblog.com, March 17, 2016.

Kathleen Swords
Concurrent Session: *Pre-empting the Challenges at Critical Ages and Stages for Third Culture Kids and Families,* FIGT Conference 2016. Retrieved from Olga Mecking's blog www.europeanmama.com, March 15, 2016.

Adult Third Culture Kids

Dr. Fanta Aw
Interviewed at FIGT Conference 2014. Retrieved from *Insights and Interviews from the 2014 Families in Global Transition (FIGT) Conference*, (p. 62), Summertime Publishing, 2015.

Mary Bassey
Ignite Session: *Stories that Cloud Our Nomadic Realities: A Closer Look at the Stereotypes that Dominate the Globalization Narrative and How We Unknowingly Reinforce Them,* FIGT Conference 2016. Retrieved from Global Living Magazine www.globallivingmagazine.com, November 29, 2016.

Paulette Bethel
FIGT Webinar 2009. Retrieved from www.pmbethel. blogs.com.

Dr. Rachel Cason
Concurrent Session: *The Evolving Third Culture Kid Profile: Research Findings on Identity and Belonging, with Practical Applications in Today's World,* FIGT Conference 2016. Retrieved from *Insights and Interviews from the 2016 Families in Global Transition (FIGT) Conference* (p.123), Summertime Publishing, 2017.

Dr. Trisha Carter and Rachel Yates
Concurrent Session: *Reaching Your Audience and Selling Your Services to Help Others Find Home,* FIGT Conference 2015. Retrieved from FIGT blog www.figt.org/blog, October 18, 2015.

Melissa Dalton-Bradford
Closing Plenary Speech: *When Grief Strikes the Global Family*, FIGT Conference 2016. Retrieved from Global Living Magazine www.globallivingmagazine.com, November 29, 2016.

Pico Iyer
Interview by Robin Pascoe: *Neither Expat nor Exile, the Globetrotting Global Soul*. Retrieved from www.telegraph.co.uk, May 9, 2004.

Maria Lombart
Retrieved from Marilyn Gardner's blog www.communicatingacrossboundariesblog.com, June 12, 2017.

Susan Murray
Panel Discussion: *When Home Spans The Globe: A Look at the Third Culture Family*, FIGT Conference 2016. Retrieved from blog www.globallivingmagazine.com, November 29, 2016.

Janneke Muyselaar-Jellema
Ignite Session: *Finding Your Voice, Your Tribe and Hearing Other Voices Through Blogging*, FIGT Conference 2017. Retrieved from FIGT blog www.figt.org/blog, May 26, 2017.

Antje Rauwerda
Literature Panel: *Many Selves at Once in Third Culture Literature,* FIGT Conference 2015. Retrieved from *Insights and Interviews from the 2015 Families in Global Transition (FIGT) Conference* (p. 122), Summertime Publishing, 2016.

Ruth Van Reken
Plenary Speech: *Enlarging Our Tents: Using Lessons from the Past to Create Space for the New,* FIGT Conference 2016. Retrieved from Marilyn Gardner's blog <u>www.communicatingacrossboundariesblog.com</u>, March 17, 2016.

Tayo Rockson
Plenary Speech: *Plenary Panel of Dudes: The Next Generation,* FIGT Conference 2015. Retrieved from *Insights and Interviews from the 2015 Families in Global Transition (FIGT) Conference,* (p. 88), Summertime Publishing, 2016.
and
Ignite Session: *Use your difference to make a difference,* FIGT Conference 2015. Retrieved from *Insights and Interviews from the 2015 Families in Global Transition (FIGT) Conference* (p. 179), Summertime Publishing, 2016.

Nina Sichel
Interviewed at FIGT Conference 2015. Retrieved from *Insights and Interviews from the 2015 Families in Global Transition (FIGT) Conference* (p. 54), Summertime Publishing, 2016.

The Concept of *Home*

Dr Janet Bennet
FIGT Conference 2008. Retrieved from www.theirrationalseason.blogspot.my/2008/03/are-you-encapsulated-or-constructive.html.

Valérie Besanceney
Interviewed at FIGT Conference 2015. Retrieved from *Insights and Interviews from the 2015 Families in Global Transition (FIGT) Conference* (p. 28), Summertime Publishing, 2016.

Lydia Foxall
Panel Discussion: *When Home Spans the Globe,* FIGT Conference 2016. Retrieved from Global Living Magazine www.globallivingmagazine.com, November 29, 2016.

Scott Keehn
Panelist at FIGT Conference 2002. Published November 5, 2002 in *The Weekly Telegraph,* London, England. Retrieved from www.figt.org/joanna_parfit

Kira Miller Fabregat
Interviewed at FIGT Conference 2010. Retrieved from *Denizen Magazine,* March 8, 2010.

Tashi Nibber
Ignite Session: *Home is an Emotional Connection - Find it Through Connections,* FIGT Conference 2015. Retrieved from *Insights and Interviews from the 2014 Families in Global Transition (FIGT) Conference,* (p.171), Summertime Publishing, 2015.

Jo Parfitt
FIGT Conference 2007. Retrieved from Jo Parfitt's DVD: *Doing Time on the Rollercoaster.*

Nina Sichel
Interviewed at FIGT Conference 2015. Retrieved from *Insights and Interviews from the 2015 Families in Global Transition (FIGT) Conference* FIGT Yearbook 2015, (p. 54), Summertime Publishing, 2016.

Julia Simens
Ignite Session: *Beloved Stranger: Hired Help or Much Loved Reference Person?* FIGT Conference 2014. Retrieved from *Insights and Interviews from the 2014 Families in Global Transition (FIGT) Conference,* (p. 150), Summertime Publishing, 2015.

Belonging

Trisha Carter
Panel Session: *Is Belonging Overrated?*
FIGT Conference 2016. Retrieved from Olga Mecking's blog www.europeanmama.com, March 15, 2016.

Elizabeth Liang
Plenary Speech: *Alien Citizen: An Earth Odyssey*. FIGT Conference 2014. Retrieved from *Insights and Interviews from the 2014 Families in Global Transition (FIGT) Conference* (p. 77), Summertime Publishing, 2015.

Matt Neigh
Opening Plenary Speech, FIGT Conference 2007.

Chris O'Shaughnessy
Plenary Speech, FIGT Conference 2016. Retrieved from Olga Mecking's blog www.europeanmama.com, March 15, 2016.

Robin Pascoe
Opening Plenary Speech, FIGT Conference 2002. Published November 5, 2002 in *The Weekly Telegraph*, London, England. Retrieved from www.figt.org/joanna_parfit.

Wilhelm Post
Opening Plenary Speech, FIGT Conference 2017. Retrieved from Mariam Ottimofiore's blog www.andthenwemovedto.com, March 27, 2017.

Rita Rosenback
Panel Discussion: *Find Your Language on the Move*, FIGT Conference 2017.

Identity

Dr Janet Bennet
Opening Plenary Speech, FIGT Conference 2007, Houston.

Myra Dumapias
Kitchen Table Conversation: *Language as Identity: its Implications for Serving the Evolving Global Family*. FIGT Conference 2014. Retrieved from *Insights and Interviews from the 2014 Families in Global Transition (FIGT) Conference* (p.162), Summertime Publishing, 2015.

Scott Keehn
FIGT Conference 2002. Published November 5, 2002, *The Weekly Telegraph*, London, England. Retrieved from www.figt.org/joanna_parfit.

Jo Parfitt
Closing Plenary Speech, FIGT Conference 2007, Houston.

Rita Rosenback
Panel Discussion: *Find Your Language on The Move*, FIGT Conference 2017. Retrieved from Jane Barron's blog www.globallygrounded.org, May 30, 2017.

Barbara Schaetti
Presentation, FIGT 2004: *Becoming an Interculturalist: Why Might an Expatriate Bother?*
Retrieved from www.figt.org.

Brittani Sonnenberg
Literature Panel: *Many Selves at Once in Third Culture Literature*, FIGT Conference 2015. Retrieved from *Insights and Interviews from the 2015 Families in Global Transition (FIGT) Conference* (p.124), Summertime Publishing, 2016.

Career and Business

Cristina Baldan and Claudia Baldini
Concurrent Session: *What Expats Can Do – To Bring Hope To the World*. FIGT Conference 2017. Retrieved from Tone Delin Indrelid's blog <u>www.theothertrail.me</u>, March 28, 2017.

Apple Gidley
Closing Plenary Speech, FIGT Conference 2011.

Kilian Kröll
Panel Discussion: *Finding Your Niche*, FIGT Conference 2017. Retrieved from Mariam Ottimofiore's blog <u>www.andthenwemovedto.com</u>, March 27, 2017.

Robin Pascoe
Opening Plenary Speech, FIGT Conference 2002. Published November 5, 2002 in *The Weekly Telegraph*, London, England. Retrieved from <u>www.figt.org/joanna_parfit</u>.

Ruth Van Reken
Plenary Speech: *Enlarging Our Tents: Using Lessons from the Past to Create Space for the New*, FIGT 2016, Amsterdam. Retrieved from Valérie Bessanceney's blog <u>www.valeriebesanceney.com</u>, May 1, 2016.

Grief and Loss

Valérie Besanceney
Interviewed at FIGT Conference 2015. Retrieved from *Insights and Interviews from the 2015 Families in Global Transition (FIGT) Conference* (p.28), Summertime Publishing, 2016.

Melissa Dalton-Bradford
Plenary Speech: *When Grief Strikes the Global Family*, FIGT Conference 2016. Retrieved from Valérie Besanceney's blog www.valeriebesanceney.com, July 20, 2016.

Doug Ota
Plenary Speech, FIGT Conference 2009. Retrieved from www.globaloutpostservices.com.

Doug Ota
Plenary Speech: *Don't Leave Without Taking Your Vitamin 'G': Why Goodbyes Are Good For You*, FIGT Conference 2015. Retrieved from Global Living Magazine www.globallivingmagazine.com, May 13, 2015.

Ruth Van Reken
Interviewed at FIGT Conference 2014. Retrieved from *Insights and Interviews from the 2014 Families in Global Transition (FIGT) Conference* (p.6), Summertime Publishing, 2015.

Tribes, Networking and Community

Dr. Fanta Aw
Plenary Speech: *Global Families and Intersections of Identities: "Ubuntu"*, FIGT Conference 2014. Retrieved from *Insights and Interviews from the 2014 Families in Global Transition (FIGT) Conference* (p.80), Summertime Publishing, 2015.

Mary Bassey
Ignite Session: *Stories that Cloud Our Nomadic Realities: A Closer Look at the Stereotypes that Dominate the Globalization Narrative and How We Unknowingly Reinforce Them*, FIGT Conference 2016. Retrieved from Jane Barron's blog <u>www.globallygrounded.org</u>, November 29, 2016.

Becky Grappo
Concurrent Session: *Cultural Complexity and Hidden Diversity: Exploring Today's TCKs*. FIGT Conference 2014. Retrieved from *Insights and Interviews from the 2014 Families in Global Transition (FIGT) Conference*, Summertime Publishing, 2015.

Claudine Hakim
Interviewed at FIGT Conference 2017. Retrieved from Jane Barron's blog <u>www.globallygrounded.com</u>, May 30, 2017.

Claudine Hakim
Concurrent Session: *Fostering Inclusive Tribes*, FIGT Conference 2017. Retrieved from Jane Barron's blog www.globallygrounded.com, May 1, 2017.

Naomi Hattaway
Plenary Speech: *Me Too! Lighting the Triangle Beacon – Why Finding Your Tribe Matters*, FIGT Conference 2017. Retrieved from Jane Barron's blog www.globallygrounded.com, May 30, 2017.

Naomi Hattaway
Plenary Speech: *Me Too! Lighting the Triangle Beacon – Why Finding Your Tribe Matters*. Retrieved from Mariam Ottimofiore's blog www.andthenwemovedto.com,
March 27, 2017.

Ray S. Leki
Plenary Speech: *The Global Family Redefined*, FIGT Conference 2014. Retrieved from *Insights and Interviews from the 2014 Families in Global Transition (FIGT) Conference* (p.73), Summertime Publishing.

Patricia Linderman
Interviewed at FIGT Conference 2015. Retrieved from *Insights and Interviews from the 2015 Families in Global Transition (FIGT) Conference* (p.59), Summertime Publishing, 2016.

Ellen Mahoney
Interviewed at FIGT Conference 2014. Retrieved from *Insights and Interviews from the 2014 Families in Global Transition (FIGT) Conference* (p.16), Summertime Publishing, 2015.

Chris O'Shaughnessy
Plenary Speech: *The Power Of Empathy*, FIGT Conference 2016. Retrieved from Olga Mecking's blog www.europeanmama.com, March 15, 2016.

Chris O'Shaughnessy
Concurrent Session: *Changing our Concept of Home to Find Hope,* at FIGT Conference 2015. Retrieved from *Insights and Interviews from the 2015 Families in Global Transition (FIGT) Conference* (p.113), Summertime Publishing, 2016.

Pam Perraud
Closing Plenary Speech, FIGT Conference 2002. Published in *The Weekly Telegraph,* November 5, 2002. Retrieved from www.figt.org/joanna_parfit.

Hannele Secchia
Interviewed at FIGT Conference 2017. Retrieved from Jane Barron's blog www.globallygrounded.com, May 1, 2017.

Jane Smith
Concurrent Session, FIGT Conference 2007, Houston.

Marielle de Spa
Interviewed at FIGT Conference 2017. Retrieved from Jane Barron's blog www.globallygrounded.com, March 28, 2017.

Sandy Thomas
Sourced at FIGT Conference 2009. Retrieved from Jo Parfitt's blog www.ExpatRollercoaster.com (now defunct).

Danau Tanu
Interviewed at FIGT Conference 2014. Retrieved from *Insights and Interviews from the 2014 Families in Global Transition (FIGT) Conference* (p.20), Summertime Publishing, 2015.

Elder Care

College-age TCKs from 1994, 2001 and 2014
Retrieved from www.globallivingmagazine.com,
May 13, 2015.

Kathleen Swords
Concurrent Session: *Pre-empting the Challenges
at Critical Ages and Stages for Third Culture Kids
and Families*, FIGT Conference 2016. Retrieved
from Olga Mecking's blog www.europeanmama.com,
March 15, 2016.

**Dr. Jill Kristal and Elizabeth Vennekens-
Kelly**
Seminar: *Forgotten Relatives*, FIGT Conference
2014. Retrieved from Sue Mannering's blog
www.expatclic.com, September 13, 2014.

Technology

College-age TCKs from 1994, 2001 and 2014
Retrieved from www.globallivingmagazine.com,
May 13, 2015.

Mariam Ottimofiore
Early Bird Forum: *Connecting With Your Online Tribe
Through Blogging When Abroad*, FIGT Conference
2017. Retrieved from Tone Indrelid's blog
www.theothertrail.me.

Grant Simens
Plenary Panel: *Plenary Panel of Dudes: The Next
Generation*, FIGT Conference 2015. Retrieved from
*Insights and Interviews from the 2015 Families
in Global Transition (FIGT) Conference*, (p.88),
Summertime Publishing, 2016.

Creativity

Alix Carnot
Concurrent Session: *Managing Dual Careers Abroad,* FIGT Conference 2017. Retrieved from Mariam Ottimofiore's blog www.andthenwemovedto.com, March 27, 2017.

Dr. Kyung Hee Kim
Concurrent Session: *Creativity and Transition: Nurturing the Creative Potential of Third Culture Kids,* FIGT Conference 2014. Retrieved from *Insights and Interviews from the 2014 Families in Global Transition (FIGT) Conference,* (p.125), Summertime Publishing, 2015.

Jo Parfitt
Concurrent Session, FIGT Conference 2001.

Ruth Van Reken
Plenary Speech: *Enlarging our Tents: Using Lessons from the Past to Create Space for the New,* FIGT Conference 2016. Retrieved from Marilyn Gardner's blog www.communicatingacrossboundariesblog.com, March 17, 2016.

Josh Sandoz
Retrieved from www.denizenmag.com, March 8, 2010.

Personal Development, Resilience and Curiosity

Dana Bachar Grossman
Retrieved from Mariam Ottimofiore's blog
www.andthenwemovedto.com, March 27, 2017.

Cristina Bertarelli
Ignite Session: *Changing Home is More than a Theory*, FIGT Conference 2015. Retrieved from *Insights and Interviews from the 2015 Families in Global Transition (FIGT) Conference* (p.194), Summertime Publishing, 2016.

Sebastien Bellin
Plenary Speech: *I Should Fear, But I Don't, So Why Do You?* Retrieved from Mariam Ottimofiore's blog www.andthenwemovedto.com, March 27, 2017.

Dr. Anne Copeland
Plenary Speech: *Are TCKs Uniquely Good at Perspective Taking? The Childhood Experience of Being Different and Its Impact on Expatriate Living*, FIGT Conference 2017. Retrieved from Jane Barron's blog www.globallygrounded.com

Melissa Dalton-Bradford
Plenary Speech: *When Grief Strikes the Global Family*, at FIGT Conference 2016. Retrieved from www.globallivingmagazine.com, November 29, 2016.

Lydia Foxall
Panel Discussion: *When Home Spans the Globe*, FIGT Conference 2016. Retrieved from www.globallivingmagazine.com, November 29, 2016.

Charles Frame, father of Ruth Van Reken
Interviewed at FIGT Conference 2014. Retrieved from *Insights and Interviews from the 2014 Families in Global Transition (FIGT) Conference* (p.7), Summertime Publishing, 2015.

Marilyn Gardner
Panel Discussion: *When Home Spans the Globe*, FIGT Conference 2016. Retrieved from Olga Mecking's blog www.europeanmama.com, March 15, 2016.

Linda A. Janssen
Interviewed at FIGT Conference 2014. Retrieved from *Insights and Interviews from the 2014 Families in Global Transition (FIGT) Conference* (p.44), Summertime Publishing, 2015.

Kilian Kröll
Sourced at FIGT Conference 2017. Retrieved from Jane Barron's blog www.globallygrounded.com, May 30, 2017.

Birgit Kuschel
Panel Discussion: *How to Use Body Language for a Happy Life at Home Worldwide,* FIGT Conference 2015. Retrieved from *Insights and Interviews from the 2015 Families in Global Transition (FIGT) Conference* (p. 163), Summertime Publishing, 2016.

Claudia Landini
Kitchen Table Conversation: *What Has Gone Right In 11 Years of Expatclic: How Intercultural Communication, Empathy and Encouragement Can Improve The Global Family Experience*. FIGT Conference 2016. Retrieved from *Insights and Interviews from The 2016 Families in Global Transition (FIGT) Conference* (p.201), Summertime Publishing 2017.

Patricia Linderman
Interviewed at FIGT Conference 2015. Retrieved from *Insights and Interviews from the 2015 Families in Global Transition (FIGT) Conference* (p.59), Summertime Publishing, 2016.

Ellen Mahoney
Concurrent Session: *Professionalizing Global Family Support for the 21st Century,* FIGT Conference 2014. Retrieved from *Insights and Interviews from the 2014 Families in Global Transition (FIGT) Conference* (p.108), Summertime Publishing, 2015.

Emmy McCarthy
Ignite Session: *Building a Global Village,* FIGT Conference 2016. Retrieved from Emmy McCarthy's blog www.emmymccarthy.com.

Doug Ota
Plenary Speech: *Don't Leave Without Taking Your Vitamin 'G': Why Goodbyes Are Good For You*. FIGT Conference 2015. Retrieved from www.globallivingmagazine.com, May 13, 2015.

Niels Ota
Plenary Panel: *Plenary Panel of Dudes: The Next Great Generation*, FIGT Conference 2015. Retrieved from www.globallivingmagazine.com, May 13, 2015.

Basma al Rawi
Kitchen Table Conversation: *Positively Curious*, FIGT Conference 2017. Retrieved from Tone Indrelid's blog www.theothertrail.me, March 28, 2017.

Ruth Van Reken
Plenary Speech: *Enlarging Our Tents: Using Lessons from the Past to Create Space for the New*, FIGT Conference 2016. Retrieved from Marilyn Gardner's blog www.communicatingacrossboundariesblog.com March 17, 2016.

Geremie Sawadogo
Concurrent Session: *AfricanX Culture: Assessing Intercultural Competence in Times of Global Change,* FIGT Conference 2015. Retrieved from *Insights and Interviews from the 2015 Families in Global Transition (FIGT) Conference* (p. 102), Summertime Publishing, 2016.

Dr. Jill Kristal and Elizabeth Vennekens-Kelly
Seminar: *Forgotten Relatives*, FIGT Conference 2014. Retrieved from www.expatclic.com September 13, 2014.

Other Tough Stuff

Sebastien Bellin
Plenary Speech: *I Should Fear, But I Don't, So Why Do You?* Retrieved from Mariam Ottimofiore's blog www.andthenwemovedto.com, March 27, 2017.

Naomi Hattaway
Plenary Speech: *Me Too! Lighting the Triangle Beacon -Why Finding Your Tribe Matters.* Retrieved from Mariam Ottimofiore's blog www.andthenwemovedto.com, March 27, 2017.

Doug Ota
Plenary Speech: *Don't Leave Without Taking Your Vitamin 'G': Why Goodbyes Are Good For You.* FIGT Conference 2015. Retrieved from www.globallivingmagazine.com, May 13, 2015.

Chris O'Shaugnessy
Interviewed at FIGT Conference 2015. Retrieved from www.taylorjoymurray.com, 22 April 2015.

Grant Simens
Plenary Panel: *Plenary Panel of Dudes: The Next Great Generation*, FIGT Conference 2015. Retrieved from www.globallivingmagazine.com, May 13, 2015.

Global Citizens

Cliff Gardner
Panel Discussion: *Finding Your Niche: Connecting a Multicultural Past to a Meaningful Present*, FIGT Conference 2017. Retrieved from <u>www.figt.org</u>, May 26, 2017.

Pico Iyer
Sourced at FIGT Conference 2004. Retrieved from *The Telegraph*, May 9, 2004.

Pico Iyer
Interviewed at FIGT Conference 2013. Retrieved from Trisha Carter's blog <u>www.cicollective.com</u>, April 2, 2013.

Claudia Landini
Kitchen Table Conversation: *What Has Gone Right in 11 Years of Expatclic: How Intercultural Communication, Empathy and Encouragement Can Improve the Global Family Experience,* FIGT Conference 2016. Retrieved from *Insights and Interviews from the 2016 Families in Global Transition (FIGT) Conference* (p.201), Summertime Publishing, 2017.

Ray S. Leki
Plenary Speech: *The Global Family Redefined*, FIGT Conference 2014. Retrieved from *Insights and Interviews from the 2014 Families in Global Transition (FIGT) Conference* (p. 72), Summertime Publishing, 2015.

Emmy McCarthy
Ignite Session: *Building a Global Village*, FIGT
Conference 2016. Retrieved from Emmy McCarthy's
blog www.emmymccarthy.com.

Doug Ota
Interviewed at FIGT Conference 2015. Retrieved
from www.uydmedia.com, July 5, 2015.

Michael Pollock
Retrieved from www.globallivingmagazine.com,
November 29, 2016.

Geremie Sawadogo
Concurrent Session: *AfricanXculture: Assessing
Intercultural Competence in Times of Global
Chance*, FIGT Conference 2015. Retrieved from
*Insights and Interviews from the 2015 Families
in Global Transition (FIGT) Conference*, (p.102),
Summertime Publishing, 2016.

Terry Anne Wilson
Retrieved from Jane Barron's blog
www.globallygrounded.com, May 30, 2017.

Diversity, Being Different

Teja Arboleda
Interviewed at FIGT Conference 2015. Retrieved from *Insights and Interviews from the 2015 Families in Global Transition (FIGT) Conference* (p.24), Summertime Publishing, 2016.

Teja Arboleda
Retrieved from Marilyn Gardner's blog www.communicatingacrossboundariesblog.com March 9, 2015.

Cristina Baldan and Claudia Landini
Concurrent Session: *What Expats Can Do – To Bring Hope to the World*, FIGT 2017. Retrieved from Tone Indrelid's blog www.theothertrail.me, March 28, 2017.

Dr. Anne Copeland
Plenary Speech: *Do TCKs Have Unique Skills? The Childhood Experience of Being Different and Its Impact on Expatriate Living*, FIGT Conference 2017. Retrieved from Tone Indrelid's blog www.theothertrail.me, March 28, 2017.

Eva László-Herbert
Interviewed at FIGT Conference 2013. Retrieved from Judy Rickatson's blog www.judyrickatson.com, April 15, 2013.

Kendra Mirasol and Charisse Kosova
Interviewed at FIGT Conference 2010. Retrieved from *Denizen Mag*, March 8, 2010.

Robin Pascoe
Sourced at FIGT Conference 2002. Retrieved from
the *Weekly Telegraph*, 2002.

Ruth Van Reken
Plenary Speech: *Enlarging Our Tents: Using
Lessons from the Past to Create Space for the
New*, FIGT Conference 2016. Retrieved from Olga
Mecking's blog www.europeanmama.com, March 15,
2016.

Chris O'Shaughnessy
Plenary Speech: *Bringing Hope To the World:
The Critical Mission of the Expat, Transient
and Cross-Cultural Community*, FIGT Conference
2016. Retrieved from Olga Mecking's blog www.
europeanmama.com, March 15, 2016.

Charity, Volunteering and Giving Back

Patricia Stokke
Concurrent Session: *Adult Third Culture Kids: Potential and Global Leaders with a Global Mindset,* FIGT Conference 2014. Retrieved from *Insights and Interviews from the 2014 Families in Global Transition (FIGT) Conference* (p. 100), Summertime Publishing, 2015.

Deborah Valentine
Concurrent Session: *The ABC and XYZ of Finding Your Tribe on Arrival — Lessons From an Active Tribe Builder.* Retrieved from Mariam Ottimofiore's blog, www.andthenwemovedto.com, March 27, 2017.

The FIGT Conference Itself

Maryam Afnan Ahmad
Interviewed at FIGT Conference 2014. Retrieved from *Insights and Interviews from the 2014 Families in Global Transition (FIGT) Conference* (p.37), Summertime Publishing, 2015.

Anonymous
Sourced at FIGT Conference 2004. Retrieved from Dr Anne Copeland's blog,
<u>www.interchangeinstitute.org</u>.

Becky Grappo
Sourced at FIGT Conference 2015. Retrieved from *Homecomings*, <u>www.figt.org/blog</u> March 2015.

Kilian Kröll
Interviewed at FIGT Conference 2015. Retrieved from *Insights and Interviews from the 2015 Families in Global Transition (FIGT) Conference* (p.23), Summertime Publishing, 2016.

Kilian Kröll
Opening remarks at FIGT Conference 2015. Retrieved from <u>www.figt.org/blog</u>, March 7, 2015.

Ellen Mahoney
Concurrent Session: *Professionalizing Global Family Support for the 21st Century,* FIGT Conference 2014. Retrieved from *Insights and Interviews from the 2014 Families in Global Transition (FIGT) Conference* (p. 109) Summertime Publishing, 2015.

Hannele Secchia
Retrieved from Jane Barron's blog, www.globallygrounded.com/blog, May 1, 2017.

Books from Summertime Publishing

by your side from inspiration to publication

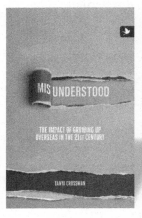

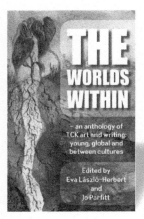

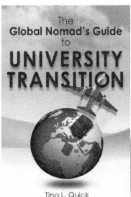

My
Moving Booklet

We all wish you very much
and wish you all the best
on your new adventure!

Expat
TEENS TALK

Peers, Parents and Professionals
offer support, advice and solutions
in response to Expat Life Challenges
as shared by Expat Teens

Dr. Lisa Pittman and Diana Smit

SLURPING SOUP
and other confusions:

B is Home

Emma Moves again

"That impresses me on my website about..." Expatriate Press

Jo Parfitt & Colleen Reichrath-Smith

a **career**
in your Suitcase

A practical guide to creating meaningful work...anywhere

4th Edition

A Global Nomad's Journey From Hurt To Healing

MORE THAN
32,000
COPIES SOLD

Letters

NEVER SENT

RUTH E. VAN REKEN

THE EMOTIONALLY
RESILIENT EXPAT

Engage, Adapt and Thrive Across Cultures

FOREWORD BY DOUG OTA

EMOTIONAL
RESILIENCE
AND THE EXPAT CHILD

Practical tips and storytelling techniques
that will strengthen the global family

UNPACK
A guide to life as an expat spouse

Lana Wimmer
Tanya Asley

TERRY ANNE WILSON
& JO PARFITT

MONDAY
MORNING
EMAILS

Six months. twelve countries. a thousand thoughts — two mothers share the journey of living a global life

---

AN
INCONVENIENT
POSTING

Retire to the
Life You Love
Practical Tools for Designing
Your Meaningful Future

Books from Expatriate Press

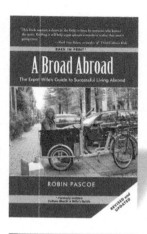

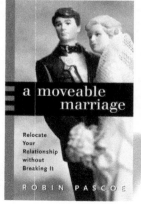

Lightning Source UK Ltd.
Milton Keynes UK
UKOW01f2223080218
317598UK00002B/192/P